Made in the USA
Monee, IL
10 October 2021

79739269R00068